The
New Lone Star Quilt
Handbook

Blanche Young
Helen Young Frost

C & T Publishing
Lafayette, California

✳ Acknowledgements _____

Our heartfelt thanks to our friends for sharing their quilts: Sandy Lawrence, Cyndi Chabot, Jeanne Scrimpsher, Pat Gilbert, Lois Horbal, Debbie Gordon and Pam Cody; including those in the Lone Star state: Kathleen McCrady, Beth Kennedy, Glennis Nokes, and especially Lynn Young, for also offering her own discoveries from teaching the Lone Star quilt.

Copyright © 1989 by Blanche Young and Helen Young Frost

Photography by Lee Karjala and Connie Johanneson

Illustration by Helen Young Frost

Published by C&T Publishing
P.O. Box 1456
Lafayette, California 94549

ISBN: 9-914881-12-4

Printed in the United States of America

✳ Contents _____

✴ Introduction _____

In the ten years since the original *Lone Star Quilt Handbook* was published, we have continued to make Lone Star quilts, exploring design variations, experimenting with fabrics and colors, and improving our construction techniques. We have taught classes at shops and conferences across the country and witnessed the creation of hundreds of wonderful Lone Star quilts.

This revised edition includes our discoveries from those years. We show more adventurous color and fabric combinations. Unusual sets and borders are displayed in the pictured quilts. We include more options for sizes of diamonds and sizes of quilts. And we share our exciting Scrap Stars; made with our streamlined methods yet utilizing many, many fabrics.

Most importantly, we include improved sewing techniques. Our original method was considered "state-of-the-art" in 1979. However, new tools for quilters such as the rotary cutter, required a new approach. We also applied some of the techniques we developed for our other books.

There is an important difference between our method and other new methods. Ours features the cutting and sewing of one pont at a time. We believe the level of interest and accuracy remains higher this way.

As before, it is our hope that this method will provide the incentive to make a quilt that might not have been attempted otherwise, and in doing so, help others experience the joy of quiltmaking.

✳ Fabric and Design

Fabric

Fabrics of 100% cotton are the quilters' choice. Avoid extremely light weight fabrics, especially for the center. A variety of prints will add more interest to the quilt. Paisleys, dots, geometric designs, and florals, large and small, all combine for an varied effect. Very large prints will lend a lacy look, especially when two are used next to each other. Stripes and strong directional designs may be used but will require special cutting.

One way to begin selecting fabrics is to find one print you like and build on that. This print can be anywhere in the star, depending on whether lighter or darker fabrics are added. Sometimes the final selection of fabrics will not even include that original choice.

You may want to wait to buy the fabric for the corners, or background, of the star until the points are completed. The points can be placed on different colors to judge their effect. Fabrics for the borders can be purchased at the same time as the fabrics for the points. Either select two or three of the fabrics for borders, or perhaps get a small amount of each of the fabrics to use for a patchwork border. One border treatment that is effective on the large quilts is using the background fabric as the first border. This helps "float" the star and keeps wide borders from dominating.

All fabrics should be rinsed and pressed before using. We endorse using spray starch while pressing to return that crispness that laundering removes. This will also stabilize the fabric during marking and sewing.

Design

Our approach to color design in the Lone Star has always involved a subtle gradation of colors. Although many antique quilts have mixed light and dark fabrics, we prefer placing the fabrics so they gradually change value or color. Mixing lights with darks can create a choppy, checkerboard effect. Sudden changes in color can form a series of bulls' eyes. A sudden change in color is effective if within the two colors there is a gradation.

We have tried to include in the color plates a variety of color treatments. Each quilt has its own personality because of the colors used.

The order of the fabrics in the star will create different designs. We have labelled three of these designs.

Reverse-Repeat Design

This is the most popular arrangement, creating a balanced, formal design. The fabrics are placed in order from the center of the star out to the widest part of each point. They then repeat, in reverse order. Each fabric is used twice in each point, except for the last, which is used once.

Reverse-Repeat

Repeat Design

This arrangement creates a sunburst effect. The contrast of the lightest fabric against the darkest can cause a pulsating effect. The fabrics are placed in order from the center of the star out to the widest part of each point. They then repeat, beginning again with the first fabric. Each fabric is used twice in each point, except for the last, which is used once.

The Repeat design has the advantage of requiring the same yardage amounts and number of diamonds of each fabric. The rows of diamonds are cut then further separated into the smaller rows.

Repeat

Radiating Design

This arrangement can give different effects, depending on the fabrics chosen. It provides the opportunity to use a wider range of colors. The fabrics are placed in order from the center of the star out to the tips. Each fabric is used once in each point.

After selecting the fabrics for the chosen arrangement, take a swatch from each and tape or glue them in order.

Special Effects

Special effects with prints are created by cutting the diamonds separately. Use a single diamond template, preferably transparent. Centering a flower or paisley motif will add to the visual impact of the quilt, especially when used in the center. Whenever possible, have two sides of the diamond parallel to the grain of the fabric for ease in sewing.

The diamonds should also be cut separately on any striped or directional prints. Stripes can be placed on the width or length of the diamond.

Even though these diamonds are cut individually, they can still be sewn in rows by taping them together. Remove the tape before pressing.

Radiating

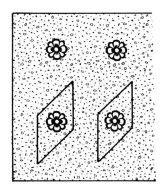

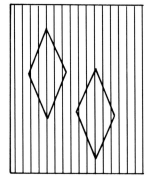

Scrap Design

The Lone Star can also be a scrap quilt. This is a scrap quilt with a difference however. It can be made in with the same methods as the planned quilts; the arrangement is somewhat planned; and the fabrics can be arranged in any of the above designs.

There are two approaches to selecting fabrics for a scrap star. For each fabric position, eight different fabrics are used. The first approach uses eight fabrics in approximately the same color and value (or darkness) in each position. The second approach uses eight fabrics in different colors but in the same value, in each position.

It's easy to select fabrics that are the same color and value. For example: eight different light tans for fabric #1; eight different medium tans for Fabric #2; eight different rust fabrics for Fabric #3; etc. They shouldn't be exactly the same color or value, of course. Somewhat darker or lighter fabrics, and slightly different shades of the colors will give a more scrappy look.

The second approach, using fabrics of the same value but different colors, is more challenging. Tans, grays, and blues could be used for the same fabric position, if they are the same value. A blue print could be mixed with brown, if they are the same value, or darkness.

Prints with several colors give the scrap stars a softened look. They sometimes help blur the colors and prevent strong rings of color. The beauty of the Scrap Lone Stars is the soft, antique look from using so many fabrics.

Reverse-Repeat

Repeat

Radiating

✴ Sewing the Star _____

Template Method

This is basically our original method of using a multiple template to mark rows of diamonds which are then cut out, sewn into a planned arrangement, and then cut apart and resewn into the points of the star. It involves marking the sewing and cutting lines of the diamonds on each fabric. It provides extremely accurate results.

Carefully cut out the template, staying close to the line. Cut the notches, lifting up the flap of cardboard to remove it. Use an ⅛ inch hole punch or large darning needle to pierce the template on the sewing line.

Each sewing layout for the various sizes of quilts will list the total number of diamonds or rows of diamonds to mark. Always mark on the wrong side of the fabric, parallel to the selvage, with the same side of the template on top.

The diamonds will be marked on each fabric. Use double sided tape on the back of the template to prevent slipping. Carefully mark around the template, keeping close to the edge. Mark in the notches and the holes. Only part of the template will be used for the short rows of diamonds. Longer rows will be marked in sections, with the template overlapping the previously marked diamonds.

Continue marking until the correct number of diamonds are marked. Use a ruler to draw a line from notch to notch. By marking this line first, it will be easier to find the small dots that indicate the sewing lines. Using the ruler, connect these dots.

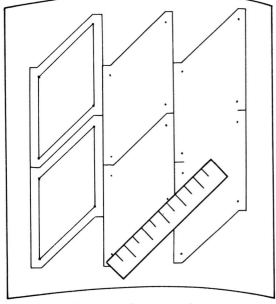

Drawing the sewing line

Cut these diamonds into rows as indicated in the sewing layouts for the quilts. Only Fabric #1 will have individual diamonds. The others are rows of diamonds; resist the temptation to cut them apart. If the fabric was folded during the marking, be sure to separate the layers before cutting. Folding will result in reversed, or mirror image, rows. If this accidently happens, cut the diamonds apart and then tape them back together in the correct direction. They will eventually be cut apart; the tape holds them in place during the sewing.

A variation on this method is to first cut the fabric into strips the correct width and then placing the template on each cut strip to add the inside markings. Several layers of fabric can be cut at a time, using scissors or the rotary cutter. Fabrics can even be folded, since the strips will be sorted before the template is used to mark the diamonds. Only cut as many layers as can be done accurately. We have redrafted the sizes of the diamonds so the width of the template would be a rounded amount. You can use any ruler to mark or cut the strips.

We have eliminated the tips of the diamond's seam allowance, to aid in the sewing stages. This does make the cutting a little more work, but will result in easier and more accurate sewing later.

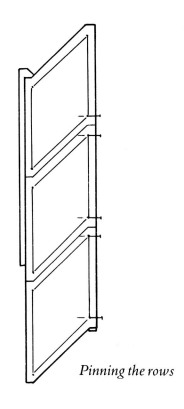

Pinning the rows

Sewing

Since these diamonds are cut and sewn in rows, they are handled much less. They will be more accurate because much of the distortion caused by handling will be eliminated.

Place the cut rows right side up, following the sewing layouts. Pin the rows together, matching the dots on the sewing lines. The notch markings will help line up the sewing line dots. Pin as shown, putting only an eighth inch of fabric on the pin, to reduce slipping. Pin all the rows together for each point.

Sew on the marked sewing lines, removing the pins just as the needle reaches them. Instead of backstitching, extend the line of stitching. Sew all the rows for one point together.

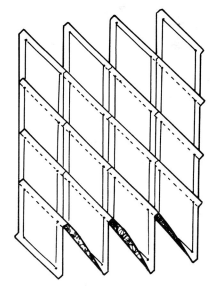

Pressing the layout

Press, with all the seams towards the outer tips of the star. Press on the back, then turn over and press gently on the front. From the back, all the marked lines should match. Cut apart on the marked cutting lines. Turn each row over in place. By aligning the edges, the rows will form a point of the star.

Again pin all the rows for each point together, before sewing. It's easy to get them out of order while sewing, unless they were pinned. If they do get mixed up, simply turn them face down and recreate the sewing layout. Pin at every seam and at each end. Pin at the dots marked on the sewing lines. Avoid excessive handling of the cut rows since the edges are on the bias.

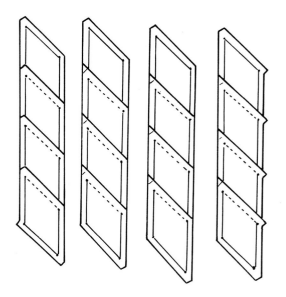

Cutting the layout

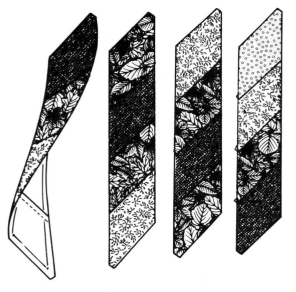

Turn to right side

Aligning the edges

Constructing the Points

Sew the rows together, with the seams as straight as possible. We know that they tend to waver as the presser foot goes over the bulk of the other seams. Avoid pulling or stretching the rows.

After sewing each row, turn and check to see if the points match. A seam that is an ⅛ inch off will cause the points to be off by a ¼ inch. If the seam is too narrow, another line of stitching right next to the first will correct it. Don't bother removing the first row of stitching. If a seam is too wide, add another line of stitching, then remove the first stitching. Don't take out the stitching first, since that will stretch the edges. When the seams have to be corrected, the whole seam does not have to be redone, only the area over the crossing seams.

Press the finished points, again with all the seams towards the outer tips of the star. Just as each diamond has two bias edges and two straight edges, so does each finished point. Press gently and avoid stretching the bias edges. The pressing diagram shows how the seams should face away from the center of the quilt. This gives a consistent look to the star, and makes quilting next to the seams uniform.

If the bias edges of the points have been stretched, it will be easy to spot when sewing the points into the star. The edges will not match; the bias edges will be longer. This can be corrected with an special type of staystitching. Unthread the sewing machine and feed the edges of the points under the presser foot while holding a finger tightly behind it. The fabric will pile up behind the foot; lift your finger every few inches to release it. Placing something behind the presser foot causes the feed mechanism to form a series of tiny ripples or pleats in the fabric. Do the entire bias edge of each point this way to return the edges to their original shape. Any fabric that has been distorted can be restored to its original shape by doing this.

Seam too narrow   *Seam too wide*

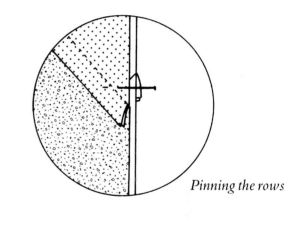

Pinning the rows

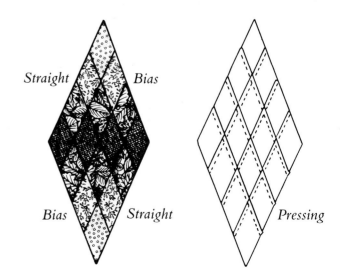

Straight *Bias*

Bias *Straight*   *Pressing*

13

Modified Template Method

This method is similar to the techniques we use for our Trip Around the World quilts. It involves using a template to measure rows of diamonds. Layers of fabrics can be cut together, and snips, or notches, are used instead of markings. It requires close attention to the size of the seam allowance.

Each sewing layout for the different designs indicates the number of diamonds and rows of diamonds that are needed. Only cut as many layers of fabrics that can be done with accuracy. Fabrics cannot be cut while folded right sides together, since this will result in reversed diamonds. Cut pieces of fabric that are approximately the needed width and layer them with the same side up. Then mark around the template and cut. Or cut the fabric into strips the exact width needed, and turn them all wrong side up before placing the template on them to mark the ends.

All of the quilts require eight rows, or multiples of eight rows, of each fabric. Quilters that are experienced with the rotary cutter usually can cut eight layers quite well. An excellent pair of scissors will also cut through this many layers. A more cautious approach is to cut only four layers at a time.

Mark around the template, as close as possible. Also mark the notches. With this method it is not necessary to mark the dots for the sewing lines. Pin the layers together if scissors are used for cutting. When the rotary cutter is used, the rule holds the layers in place during cutting. Cut out the rows of diamonds, snipping the notches ¼ inch.

While using the rotary cutter, a clear ruler can be placed over the template during cutting. This would eliminate any marking. The small wheel rotary cutter can even be used to snip the notches.

Again, the ends of the rows take time to cut, but while help contribute to ease and accuracy during the sewing.

Place the cut rows in the proper sewing layout. No pinning is necessary with this method, since the notches indicate the placement of the rows during the sewing.

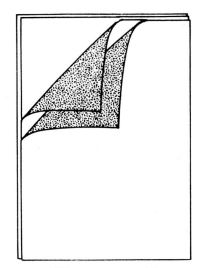

All layers wrong side up

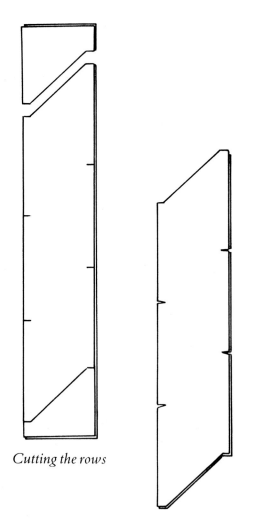

Cutting the rows

Snipping the notches

14

Sew the rows together, using exactly ¼ inch seam allowances. Match the snips as you sew. The blunted ends of the rows help establish the correct seam allowance and offer a better edge for the sewing machine to grasp. Sew all the rows for each point together.

Press, with all the seams towards the outer tips of the star. Place each sewn layout face down. Using the template, draw a cutting line. Or use a rule to line up the edges of the outer diamonds to establish where to cut. Cut the sewn layout into rows.

Turn each row over, in place. Align the edges into the points. Pin the rows for each point together before sewing to keep them in order. Place each pin ¼ inch in from the edge, right next to the seam. Pin to the next row, exactly where the seams will intersect.

Pin and sew these rows into points, using a consistent ¼ inch seam allowance. Follow the directions in the Template Method section for constructing the points.

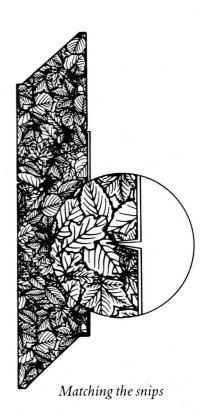

Matching the snips

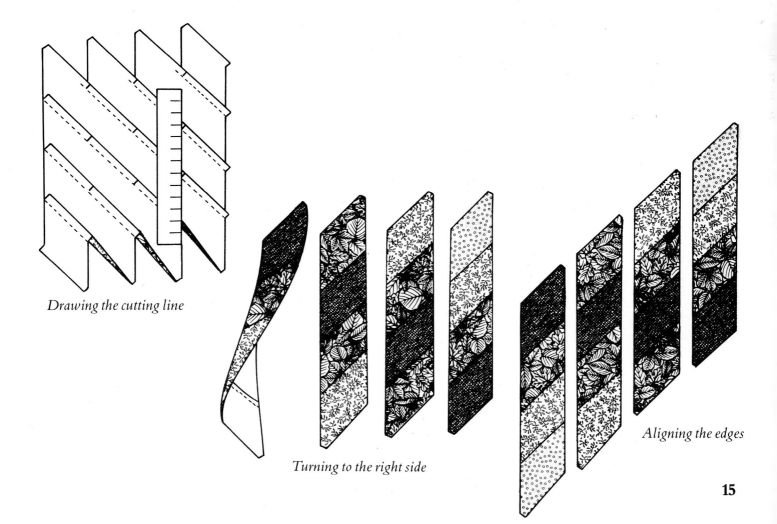

Drawing the cutting line

Turning to the right side

Aligning the edges

15

Strip Method

This new method, although it appears easy and carefree, actually requires very close attention to cutting and sewing. Strips are cut and joined in an arrangement; strips are then cut from this and the excess fabric is removed to form rows of diamonds which can then be sewn into points.

The sewing layouts for each of the quilt designs indicate the number and size of the strips to cut. The strips can be cut by using the rotary cutter and ruler, or by marking the width and using scissors.

Only cut as many layers as can be done accurately. Fabric can be left folded since the strips will be sorted before they are sewn. It's easier to cut the fabrics into the width needed and then trim the ends to the correct length.

Fold each strip in half to find the center. Sew into the layout, matching the center creases. It's even possible to chain piece these strips. Sew the first two strips for each point, without clipping the threads between. Then add the third strip to all of the points. Continue in this manner until all the strips are sewn into the layouts. Press the strips towards the fabric that will be the outer tips of the star.

The success of this method depends on the accuracy of the ¼ inch seam allowance. If the seam is too large, the entire unit becomes condensed. Although we have allowed an extra half inch at the ends of the strips, the unit may not be able to yield the correct number of rows. If the seam is too small, the entire unit become enlarged. If this happens, extra strips of fabric may have to be removed from between the cut rows.

Place the sewn units face down. The cutting line must be at a 45 degree angle to the seams. Do this very carefully since this establishes the angle for the finished diamonds.

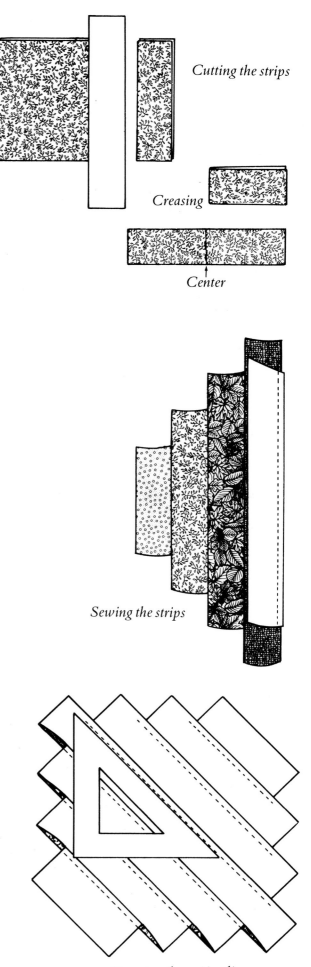

Cutting the strips

Creasing

Center

Sewing the strips

Drawing the cutting line

1. Antique Lone Star, 86″ x 92″ (Collection of Helen Young Frost.)

2. Antique Scrap Lone Star, 90″ x 90″ (Collection of Helen Young Frost.)

4. Radiant Star, 45″ x 45″, by Blanche Young.

3. Lone Star, 60″ x 60″, by Lynn Young.

5. Lone Star wall quilt, Reverse-Repeat design, 45″ x 45″, by Blanche Young.

6. Lone Star wall quilt, Repeat design, 45″ x 45″, by Blanche Young.

7. Lone Star quilt, Radiating design, 102″ x 102″, by Jeanne Scrimpsher.

8. Lone Star wall quilt, 50″ x 50″, by Sandy Lawrence.

9. Octagon Lone Star wall quilt by Pat Gilbert.

10. Broken Star, 97″ x 97″, by Blanche Young.

11. Lone Star, 94″ x 96″, by Cyndi Chabot.

12. Baby Lone Star, 45″ x 45″, by Blanche Young.

13. Broken Star, 105″ x 105″, by Lynn Young.

14. Lone Star with Applique, 85″ x 85″, by Lynn Young.

Use the rotary cutter and a ruler to cut the rows. If you are using scissors, use a ruler to measure the correct width and mark a cutting line. The first cut, or line, must be one half inch away from the inside edge. Cut into the same size strip as before.

Turn these rows over to the right side, leaving them in the same order. Align the edges to form a point. At this stage, the point is very ragged since there is excess fabric on the ends of some of the diamonds. Without disturbing the order of the rows, remove the excess pieces. For those of you that detest ripping out stitches, do not be dismayed. Simply clip the threads every half inch and the thread on the other side will pull out easily. The amount of time saved by cutting strips with squared ends is well worth the few minutes that removing these little pieces will take.

Pin and sew these rows into points, using a consistent ¼ inch seam allowance. Follow the directions in the Template Method section for constructing the points.

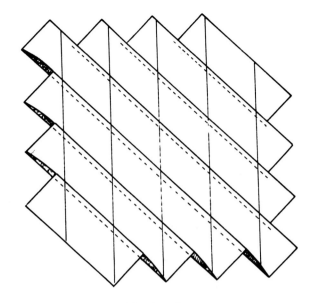

Cutting the rows

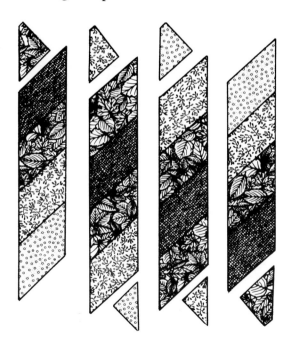

Removing the excess fabric

Forming a point

21

Scrap Lone Star

The Scrap Lone Star has an charming antique look from the many fabrics and the random placement of those fabrics. And they are fun to make! The Scrap Lone Star can be made with any of the three construction methods we have presented. The sewing is the same, just the placement of fabrics and the arrangement of the rows of diamonds differ.

Fabric requirements are difficult to specify. So much depends on the shape of the fabric used. Some quilters prefer leaving as long a piece as possible when cutting for a project. Others use up their pieces from selvage to selvage. And we're all familiar with those truly odd shaped pieces in our fabric supply! Since the Scrap Lone Star is made by cutting strips or rows, it isn't feasible to use very small scraps.

You do not have to use the Strip Method to make the Scrap Lone Star, yet the cutting instructions for that method will tell the approximate sizes the pieces of fabric need to be.

Follow the instructions for the Construction Method of your choice. Keep in mind that the number of fabrics will be eight times as many. There will be eight different fabrics for Fabric #1; eight for #2; etc. On the Reverse Repeat arrangement, the same fabrics can be used on both inner and outer sides of the points, or all different fabrics can be selected. The more fabrics used will insure less chance of having duplicates next to each other.

There are two approaches to fabric arrangement. The fabrics for each position in the star can be the same color and value; or the same value but different colors. Eight different light blues could be used for Fabric #1; eight different medium blues could be used for Fabric #2; Eight darker blues could be used for Fabric #3; etc. Each fabric position has fabrics that are approximately the same color and darkness. The second approach would have eight different light fabrics for Fabric #1 (perhaps blues, grays, and greens); eight different medium fabrics for Fabric #2 (medium blues, grays, greens, and even rust); and eight different fabrics for Fabric #3 (navy, browns, and black). The star design would still emerge if the fabrics continue to change value as they change position.

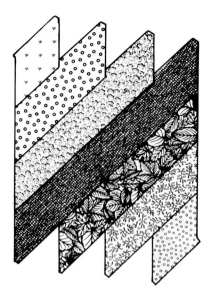

Different fabrics

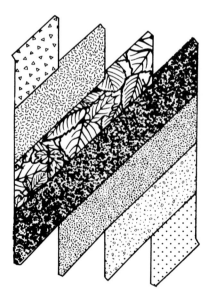

It's fun to blur the distinction between the rows by using fabrics that have more than one color in them. If the first row is pink and the next is blue, using a pink and blue fabric in either of the rows will blend the two rows together. However, if you prefer seeing the definite rings of diamonds that form the star, use fabrics that are very close in color and value in each of the different fabric positions.

The scrap effect is created by making eight different points, but mixing up the cut rows from each point before they are sewn back together. Using the method of your choice, sew the various fabrics into the sewing layout.

Each point will be different at this stage. Press the seams towards one direction, and then the other. This will allow the seams to flip easily which ever way they need to face. Cut into rows, following the directions of the method of your choice.

Keeping the rows in order, turn to the right side. Number them from left to right and set them aside, keeping them in order. Cut the next sewn unit into the rows of diamonds. Turn the rows to the right side, in order, and place them on top of the other cut rows. Continue to cut the units into rows and stack them in order. It's important to keep the rows in order, since the placement of lights and darks within each row is different.

Now the different points can be made from the cut rows. Take a row from the first stack for the first row of the point. Take any row from the second stack for the second row of the point. Take a row from the third stack for the third row of the point. This involves some "rummaging" through the stack to find a row that works well next to the previous row. After each point is laid out, it can be stacked and set aside for sewing. Inevitably, there will be some diamonds of the same fabrics next to each other. We try to avoid this, but a few duplicates will add charm to the quilt.

Sometimes it's necessary to turn the row upside down to have a better arrangement. Pressing the seams both ways allows this.

Sew the rows into points. The points should be arranged and rearranged if necessary, to avoid the same fabrics touching each other.

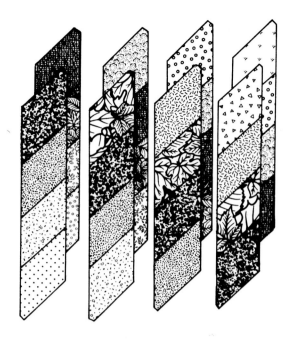

Stacking the rows

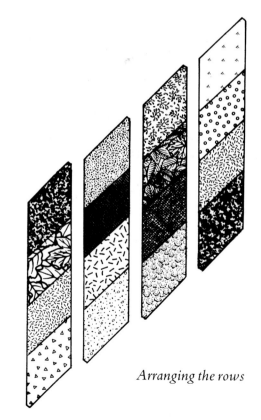

Arranging the rows

Radiant Star

The Radiant Star in Plate 4 is a simple variation of the Reverse-Repeat design. Not to be confused with the Radiating arrangement, this star has rows of diamonds that radiate outward from the center of the star, instead of concentric rings of diamonds. It's particularly effective when the last fabric (in the center of the point) contrasts strongly with the other fabrics.

Follow the directions of the Reverse-Repeat arrangement for any of the quilts. After cutting the sewn units into rows of diamonds, reverse the order of the rows before turning them right side up. When they are turned over, the diamonds will form the outward radiating effect. This design is only effective with the Reverse-Repeat arrangement, since the same fabric needs to be on both sides of the center fabric.

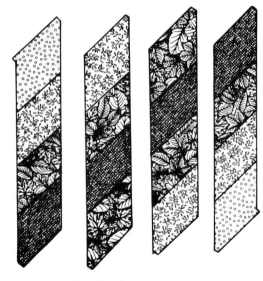

Cutting the rows

Forming the point

24

✳ Finishing the Quilt

Joining the Points

Sew the points into pairs, the pairs into halves, and then join the halves into the star. Pin carefully, angling the pins with the seams.

A bias edge will always be sewn to a straight grain edge when joining the points. By sewing from the center out, this bias edge will always be on the bottom. This will take advantage of the sewing machine's tendency to pull, or drag, on the top layer while easing in the bottom layer.

To insure a perfect center, and a flat star, some preparation before sewing is necessary. Check to see if the points are actually 45 degrees. Handling the points may have stretched the tips until they are too "pointy". Use a 45 degree triangle and mark a new sewing line, if necessary. Or place two points together to see if they form a 90 degree angle. Each pair of points will have to form 90 degree angles in order for the star to be flat. Either mark new sewing lines, or note the amount of seam allowance that should be sewn. Usually it is just the tips of the points, not the entire point, that needs to have a slightly deeper seam.

Sew from the center out, stopping and backstitching ¼ inch from the outside edges. This last ¼ inch needs to be free in order to set in the background pieces.

When joining the pairs, place the seams away from the center to reduce the bulk. Join the two halves, sewing first just across the center an inch or two. With the center matched, sew from the center out. Turn the star over to sew from the center out on the other side.

Some people prefer pressing all the joining seams open. This distributes the bulk of the seams evenly.

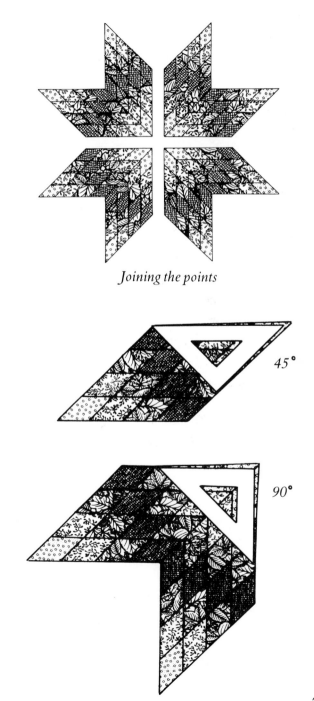

Joining the points

45°

90°

25

Background

The background of the star is formed by piecing in squares and triangles. Using all triangles will make an octagon shaped star; using all squares will create an interesting star that can be square by adding additional pieces of background.

Since slight differences in seam allowances will result in different sizes stars, it's necessary to measure the finished points to obtain the sizes to cut for the background pieces. We want your corners to fit your star, not our measurements.

Always measure the straight edge of the points. The bias edges will measure larger if they have been stretched during the handling. The straight edges will give the correct measurement; the bias edges will be eased in to fit.

Measure the points from the inside seam to the end of the sewing line. Stars constructed with the Template Method will have a dot at the end of the sewing line. The stars made with the other methods will not; simply measure to the spot where the ¼ inch seams will intersect.

Add ¼ inch seam allowances to this measurement and cut four squares. Fold one of these squares in half diagonally and use it to make a pattern for the triangles. Add a ¼ inch seam allowance beyond the fold. Or simply pin the folded square to the background fabric, using it as a pattern piece. Place the diagonal fold along the straight of the grain to avoid having bias edges on the outside of the star. The long edge of the triangle should be placed on the straight of either the crosswise or lengthwise grain. Doing two each way will keep the grain of the triangles consistent with the grain lines of the corner pieces. This is important if there is a distinct grain line or pattern to the background fabric. Cutting a square in half diagonally will use less fabric, and can be done if fabric is short, but the star will be harder to border because of the bias edges.

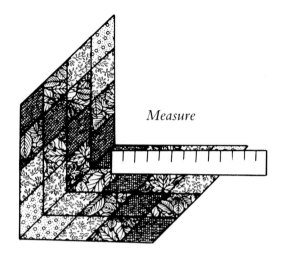

Measure

Cut background pieces as shown. Placing the triangles into a square will yield two on the crosswise grain and two on the lengthwise grain. The corner squares for the wall quilts will fit next to the large square of triangles. The squares for the other sizes will have to be placed along the length of the fabric.

Sew in the triangles first, then the squares. The last ¼ inch of the seams joining the points must be left unsewn in order to set in the background pieces. Sew with the star on the bottom and the background piece on top. Place it on the point, pinning at the ends of the sewing lines and in between. The seams joining the points should be flipped away from the needle. Sew up to that pin, backstitch one stitch, then raise the needle and presser foot. Flip the underneath seams back, then reinsert the needle. With the needle down and the presser foot up, pivot the background piece to the other side. Lower the presser foot, backstitch one stitch, then continue sewing the other side of the piece. This second edge is the straight side of the point and doesn't require as much pinning. Sewing up to a seam, then moving it before sewing on the other side of it allows the setting in of pieces on the sewing machine.

Some quilters prefer adding the background pieces in two steps. Sewing from the inside corner out, they sew one side, then the other.

The seams will want to lay towards the corners. If they show through the background fabric, they should be pressed back towards the points.

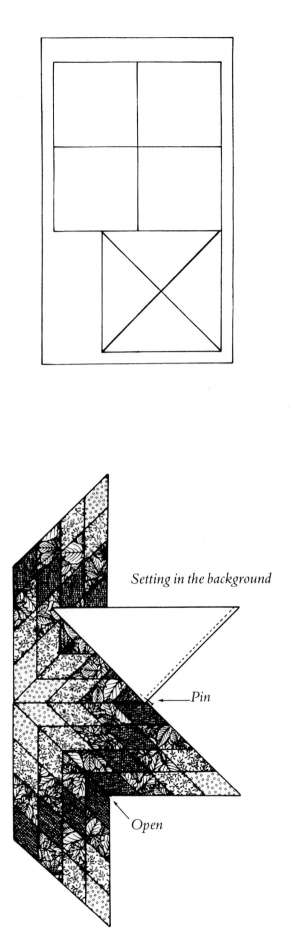

Setting in the background

Pin

Open

Borders

Borders will not only enlarge the quilt, they will provide a suitable frame for the star design. We offer some possible border treatments here and the pictured quilts will suggest many more. We list sizes of borders that certain fabric amounts will yield to enable you to purchase fabric for the borders. After the star portion of the quilt is finished, you can then design the appropriate border treatment.

One very effective approach is to first border the star with the same fabric as the background. This makes the star look larger and gives it a floating effect. It can also be adjusted to allow a patchwork border to fit the quilt.

The fabric amounts allow for piecing once on each side of the quilt. Solid borders should not be pieced if at all possible. Double the yardage amounts to allow for this.

The corners of the borders can be pieced with small squares or the borders can have mitered corners. Yardage amounts allow for either.

Patchwork borders can be planned on paper by using a diamond template without seams. The design on paper will be the same size as the finished border.

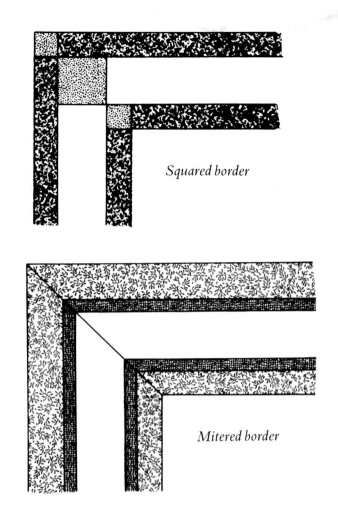

Squared border

Mitered border

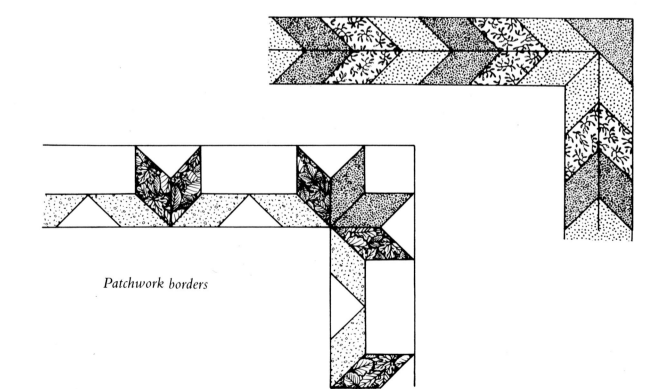

Patchwork borders

28

Mitered Border

Measure across the center of the quilt to find the length of the border. For mitered borders add the finished width size to the measurement. For multiple borders, sew the various strip together first and then handle as one piece. Mark the finished length of the quilt on the border. Then mark the diagonal seam from this point. Either fold the border and crease it, or use a draftman's triangle to mark the 45 degree angle of the seam.

Always mark the center of the borders so they can be placed correctly on the quilt.

Pin the borders to the quilt and sew from the angled line to the line on the other end. This diagonal line will be exactly ¼ inch from the edge of the quilt. After sewing all the sides to the quilt, sew the diagonal seams. Sew from the outside in towards the quilt. This helps prevent the seam from stretching since it is on the bias.

Squared Borders

Measure the quilt to determine the length of the first border. The lengths of any subsequent borders can be figured by adding the widths of the previous borders. Each border is added separately. Sew the corner squares to the top and bottom borders. Sew the side borders to the quilt, then add the top and bottom borders.

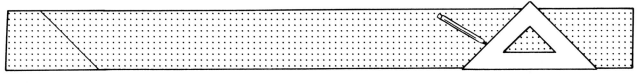

Diagonal seam

Quilting

The Lone Star is a wonderful showcase for quilting. Designs can be as elaborate as the Wreath of Roses design or as simple as parallel lines. The star portion of the quilt is quilted first, then the background areas. We have had students make the Lone Star as their very first quilt; their learning stitches are all hidden in the patchwork and their practiced, uniform stitching is displayed in the background pieces.

The diamonds themselves can be outlined, by quilting along the seamline, or be quilted ¼ inch in from the seams in the traditional style. The larger diamonds can be quilted twice, ¼ inch away from the seam and again ¾ of an inch away from the seam. There will be a small diamond centered in each larger diamond this way.

One style of quilting that will visually make smaller diamonds in each larger diamonds is to cross each diamond, parallel to the seam lines, with rows of stitching. Additional quilting next to the seams can be added to the large diamonds. Concentric stars can be formed by quilting half-way between the seams, following the shape of the star.

Any straight line quilting can be marked with a ruler and chalk or pencil. More elaborate designs should be marked using a template or stencil on top or tracing the designs through the fabrics.

Seam the backing pieces together allowing for at least two extra inches on all sides. The Lone Star quilts well in either a frame or a hoop. The larger round or oval standing hoops work especially well since they will accommodate an entire point at a time. Baste all the layers together before quilting on a hoop. Any extra fullness in the quilt should be distributed evenly in every point, by basting along the joining seams.

Begin and end every line of quilting by tying a small knot and popping through the fabric into the batting. Take small, even stitches. Always try to quilt on the side of the seam without the seam allowances.

Although it is customary to quilt from the center out on most quilts, that will cause some problems on the Lone Star. There is a tendency for the very center to poke out because there are so many seams converging there. Beginning every line of quilting there aggravates this problem. It needs rows of quilting crossing the center to keep it flat.

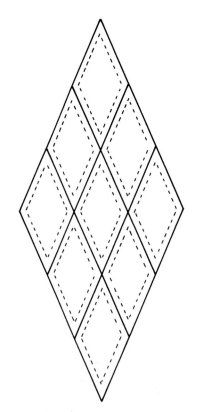

Traditional quilting

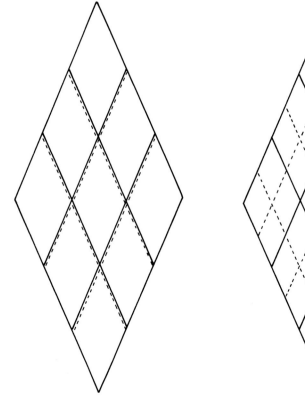

Outline quilting

Fractured diamond

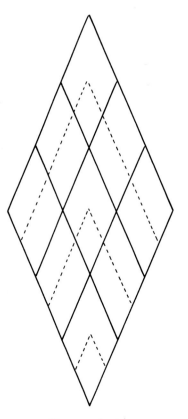

Concentric stars

Binding

This is a practical and attractive binding. The fabric is doubled for strength and the bias will give a smooth, rolled effect. A little batting filling the binding will help it wear and look better.

Fold the fabric by lining up the cut edge with the selvage. Make the strips easier to cut by doubling the folded edge. Cut strips, parallel to the fold. The first strip, since the fabric is doubled, should be 2 inches wide. Cut the rest of the fabric into 4 inch wide strips.

Sew these strips together with ½ inch seams. Press the seams open and trim them to ¼ inch. Fold the strips in half lengthwise and press. Being careful not to stretch the fabric, sew the raw edges together, using slightly less than a ¼ inch seam allowance. This helps stabilize the binding while sewing it to the quilt. Begin this staystitching twelve inches from the end.

Leaving those twelve inches free, sew the binding to the quilt. Start away from the corners, and sew without pulling on the binding. Stop stitching ¼ inch away from each corner and backstitch. Lift the needle and presser foot and form a ½ inch pleat in the binding. Reinsert the needle on the other side of the pleat, and using the needle to hold the layers in place, pivot the entire quilt. Lower the presser foot and continue sewing.

Stop sewing about twelve inches away from the starting point. The ends of the binding can be stitched together by removing some of the staystitching. Tuck the binding inside the short open end and mark, allowing for ¼ inch seams. Cut off the excess, then seam the ends together. Fold the binding and finish attaching to the quilt.

Bring the folded edge of the binding to the back of the quilt. Overlap the binding in the corners, forming the mitered effect as in the front. Blindstitch in place, pinning or basting first.

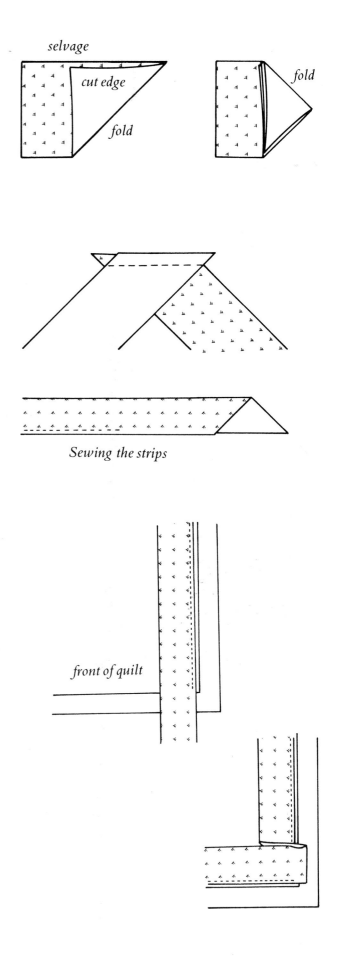

Sewing the strips

front of quilt

✳ The Quilts _____

About the Quilt Sizes

The finished size of the Lone Star quilt is determined by three factors; the size of the diamonds, the number of diamonds, and the amount of borders. We offer instructions for small wall quilts to large bed quilts; diamonds range from the tiny two inch to the generous three inch.

When we introduced our original book at Houston's Quilt Festival '79, we overheard a quilter comment, "Well, no wonder their quilts are easier; look at those great big diamonds!" Yet moments later someone walked by and said "Oh, I could never make that quilt; the diamonds are just too small!"

So now there is a choice of size of diamonds for quilts of approximately the same size. Using seven fabrics and the medium diamond will make the same size star as using the small diamond with eight fabrics. And for those true traditionalists, we include a large star of the smallest diamonds, which uses nine fabrics.

We have eliminated the extra large 3½ inch diamond that we used in the original book. The quilt of six fabrics will use the 3 inch diamond. With an approximately 64 inch star, it's ready for some of the more involved border treatments.

We have even changed the size for the Broken Star to a slightly smaller diamond. The star quilts are so much more attractive when most of the star design is on the top of the bed; they lose impact when too much of the star is off the sides of the bed.

The most important development in our method was to redraft the diamonds so the width of the template is an even measurement. The tiny diamond actually measures a finished 2⅛ inch, yet the width of that template is now a nice even 2 inches. This allows the strips for the points to be cut with any ruler you might already have. The medium diamond actually finishes at 2¾ inch; the strips are cut 2½ inch. The small diamond measures 2⅜ inch; these strips are cut 2¼ inches. The large diamond is 3⅛ inch; the strips are cut 2¾ inches wide. Remember, the diamond measurement is the finished length of the sides of the diamond; the strip measurement is the width of the template with seam allowances.

All the strips for the star can be cut first, even when using the template methods for constructing the star. Refer to the cutting instructions for the Strip Method for the sizes of these strips. Then continue to follow the instructions for either of the Template Methods.

The Strip Method cutting instructions will also tell the size of fabrics or scraps needed for each point of the Scrap Lone Star.

About the Yardage Amounts

Since these methods utilize rows of diamonds or strips of fabric, the fabric required is more than would be needed if the same number of diamonds were cut individually. Since two edges of each diamond are on the bias of the fabric, it is very important that the other two edges be placed on the lengthwise grain of the fabric. Even the crosswise grain has some stretch. Our yardage amounts are figured with the rows and strips cut with the lengthwise grain. This sometimes results in excess fabric widthwise. This can be used for smaller quilts or for patchwork borders.

Although the Lone Star can be striking with simple background and border treatments, it also lends itself to more complicated arrangements. *Solitaire Star* gives the illusion of escaping from the borders; *Lone Star Octagon* is set on point; the points in *Sunrise Star* are edged with a stripe before the background is added; and Lois Horbal's wonderful *Scrap Lone Star* in Plate 18 is set as a square within a square. We hope you will find inspiration in one of the pictured quilts and expand upon the design.

The yardage amounts for the finishing of the quilt allow for the star to be square, and border amounts are for each different border. Be sure to add additional amounts for backing and binding if your star is going to differ greatly in size from those listed.

Border fabric amounts require piecing once on each side of the quilt. Double the amount to avoid piecing. Borders can be cut on the crosswise grain for the smaller wall quilts. All other border amounts are for the lengthwise grain.

The quilts with six and nine diamonds per row are 65 inches before borders; we've allowed border and backing fabrics up to a 90 inch size. The quilts with seven and eight diamonds in each row are 68 inches before borders; we've allowed border and backing fabrics up to a 108 inch size.

Small Lone Star Wall Quilt

Quilt Size–22″ x 22″
Template–Tiny
Diamonds per row–3
Strip Width–2″

Reverse-Repeat Design Cutting Instructions

Fabric	Amount	Template Methods		Strip Method	
		Rows to Cut	Diamonds in Each	Strips to Cut	Size 2″ x
1	¼ yard	16	1	16	6″
2	¼	16	2	16	9″
3	⅜	8	3	8	11½″

Repeat Design Cutting Instructions

Fabric	Amount	Template Methods Cut 8 rows of 3 diamonds from each fabric — Separate into smaller rows of diamonds (Diamonds in each)	Strip Method Cut 8 pieces in each size 2″ x
1	⅜ yard	1 / 2	6″ / 9″
2	of	2 / 1	9″ / 6″
3	each	3	11½″

Radiating Design Cutting Instructions

Fabric	Amount	Template Methods Cut 8 rows from each fabric (Diamonds in each)	Strip Method Cut 8 strips from each fabric 2″ wide x
1 & 5	¼ yard	1	6″
2 & 4	¼	2	9″
3	⅜	3	11½″

Sewing Layouts

Template Methods   **Strip Method**

Background–½ yard
Borders–½ yard
Backing–1 yard
Binding–½ yard

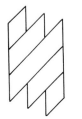
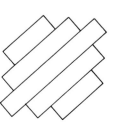

Lone Star Wall Quilt

Quilt Size–34″ x 34″
Template–Small
Diamonds per row–4
Strip Width–2¼″

Reverse-Repeat Design Cutting Instructions

Fabric	Amount	Template Methods		Strip Method	
		Rows to Cut	Diamonds in Each	Strips to Cut	Size 2¼″ x
1	¼ yard	16	1	16	6½″
2	⅜	16	2	16	10″
3	½	16	3	16	13″
4	½	8	4	8	16″

Repeat Design Cutting Instructions

Fabric	Amount	Template Methods	Strip Method
		Cut 8 rows of 4 diamonds from each fabric	Cut 8 pieces in each size
		Separate into smaller rows of diamonds (Diamonds in each)	2¼″ x
1	½ yard	1 / 3	6½″ / 13″
2	of	2 / 2	10″ / 10″
3	each	3 / 1	13″ / 6½″
4		4	16″

Radiating Design Cutting Instructions

Fabric	Amount	Template Methods	Strip Method
		Cut 8 rows from each fabric	Cut 8 strips from each fabric
		(Diamonds in each)	2¼″ x
1 & 7	¼ yard	1	6½″
2 & 6	⅜	2	10″
3 & 5	½	3	13″
4	⅝	4	16″

Sewing Layouts

Template Methods **Strip Method**

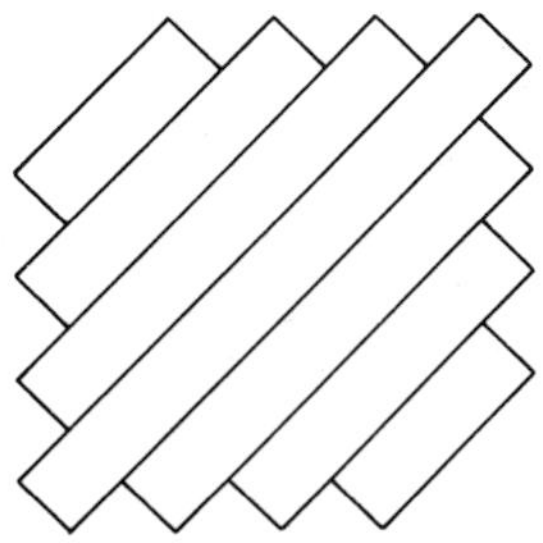

Background–¾ yard
Borders–½ yard
Backing–1¼ yards
Binding–¾ yard

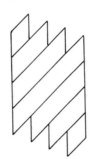

15. *Sunrise Star*, 95″ x 95″, by Blanche Young.

16. *Solitaire Star*, 100″ x 100″, by Blanche Young.

17. *Lone Star Octagon*, 97″ x 97″, pieced by Ruth Aulds, Flo Cochran, Mary Holt, Connie Hufnagel, Marge Kelly, Beth Kennedy, Modena Lyons, Kathleen McCrady, Phyllis Todaro, Lorre Weidlich: quilted by Kathleen McCrady.

18. Lone Star, 100″ x 100″, by Lois Horbal.

19. Octagon Scrap Lone Star wall quilt,
50″ x 50″, by Blanche Young.

20. Scrap Lone Star wall quilt, 45″ x 45″,
by Blanche Young.

21. Scrap Lone Star baby quilt, 46″ x 46″, by Helen Young.

22. Scrap Lone Star wall quilt, 45″ x 45″, by Blanche Young; machine quilted by Dalene Thomas.

23. Scrap Lone Star, 98″ x 98″, by Blanche Young.

24. *Texas Sesquicentennial Star*, 70″ x 70″, by Beth Kennedy.

25. Broken Star top, 85″ x 85″, by Debbie Gordon.

26. Christmas wreath by Glennis Nokes; wall quilt (on table) by Helen Young Frost.

Lone Star Baby Quilt

Quilt Size – 42″ x 42″
Template – Small
Diamonds per row – 5
Strip Width – 2¼″

Reverse-Repeat Design Cutting Instructions

Fabric	Amount	Template Methods		Strip Method	
		Rows to Cut	Diamonds in Each	Strips to Cut	Size 2¼″ x
1	¼ yard	16	1	16	6½″
2	⅜	16	2	16	10″
3	½	16	3	16	13″
4	½	16	4	16	16″
5	⅝	8	5	8	19″

Repeat Design Cutting Instructions

Fabric	Amount	Template Methods	Strip Method
		Cut 8 rows of 5 diamonds from each fabric	Cut 8 pieces in each size
		Separate into smaller rows of diamonds (Diamonds in each)	2¼″ x
1	⅝ yard	1 / 4	6½″ / 16″
2	of	2 / 3	10″ / 13″
3	each	3 / 2	13″ / 10″
4		4 / 1	16″ / 6½″
5		5	19″

Radiating Design Cutting Instructions

Fabric	Amount	Template Methods	Strip Method
		Cut 8 rows from each fabric	Cut 8 strips from each fabric
		(Diamonds in each)	2¼″ x
1 & 8	¼ yard	1	6½″
2 & 7	⅜	2	10″
3 & 6	½	3	13″
5	⅝	4	16″

Sewing Layouts

Template Methods   **Strip Method**

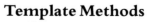

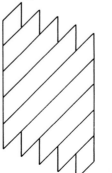
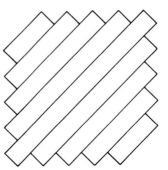

Background – 1¼ yards
Borders – ¾ yard
Backing – 3 yards
Binding – 1 yard

Lone Star Quilt

Quilt Size–65″ x 65″
Template–Large
Diamonds per row–6
Strip Width–2¾″

Reverse-Repeat Design Cutting Instructions

Fabric	Amount	Template Methods		Strip Method	
		Rows to Cut	Diamonds in Each	Strips to Cut	Size 2¾″ x
1	¼ yard	16	1	16	7½″
2	⅜	16	2	16	11½″
3	½	16	3	16	15½″
4	⅝	16	4	16	19″
5	¾	16	5	16	23″
6	⅞	8	6	8	27″

Repeat Design Cutting Instructions

Fabric	Amount	Template Methods	Strip Method
		Cut 8 rows of 6 diamonds from each fabric	Cut 8 pieces in each size
		Separate into smaller rows of diamonds (Diamonds in each)	2¾″ x
1	⅞ yard	1 / 5	7½″ / 22½″
2	of	2 / 4	11½″ / 19″
3	each	3 / 3	15½″ / 15½″
4		4 / 2	19″ / 11½″
5		5 / 1	23″ / 7½″
6		6	27″

Radiating Design Cutting Instructions

Fabric	Amount	Template Methods	Strip Method
		Cut 8 rows from each fabric	Cut 8 strips from each fabric
		(Diamonds in each)	2¾″ x
1 & 11	¼ yard	1	7½″
2 & 10	⅜	2	11½″
3 & 9	½	3	15½″
4 & 8	⅝	4	19″
5 & 7	¾	5	23″
6	⅞	6	27″

Sewing Layouts

Template Methods

Strip Method

Background – 2 yards
Borders – 1¼ yards
Backing – 5 yards
Binding – 1¼ yards

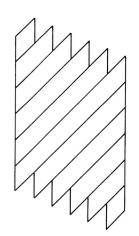

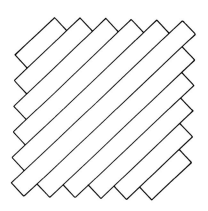

Lone Star Quilt

Quilt Size – 68″ x 68″
Template – Medium
Diamonds per row – 7
Strip Width – 2½″

Reverse-Repeat Design Cutting Instructions

Fabric	Amount	Template Methods		Strip Method	
		Rows to Cut	Diamonds in Each	Strips to Cut	Size 2½″ x
1	¼ yard	16	1	16	7″
2	⅜	16	2	16	10½″
3	½	16	3	16	14″
4	⅝	16	4	16	17½″
5	¾	16	5	16	21″
6	⅞	16	6	16	24½″
7	1	8	7	8	28″

Repeat Design Cutting Instructions

Fabric	Amount	Template Methods	Strip Method
		Cut 8 rows of 7 diamonds from each fabric	Cut 8 pieces in each size
		Separate into smaller rows of diamonds (Diamonds in each)	2½″ x
1	1 yard	1 / 6	7″ / 24½″
2	of	2 / 5	10½″ / 21″
3	each	3 / 4	14″ / 17½″
4		4 / 3	17½″ / 14″
5		5 / 2	21″ / 10½″
6		6 / 1	24½″ / 7″
7		7	28″

Radiating Design Cutting Instructions

Fabric	Amount	Template Methods	Strip Method
		Cut 8 rows from each fabric	Cut 8 strips from each fabric
		(Diamonds in each)	2½″ x
1 & 13	¼ yard	1	7″
2 & 12	⅜	2	10½″
3 & 11	½	3	14″
4 & 10	⅝	4	17½″
5 & 9	¾	5	21″
6 & 8	⅞	6	24½″
7	1	7	27½″

Sewing Layouts

Background–2⅛ yards
Borders–1½ yards
Backing–9 yards
Binding–1½ yards

Template Methods

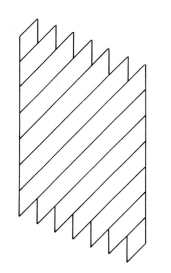

Strip Method

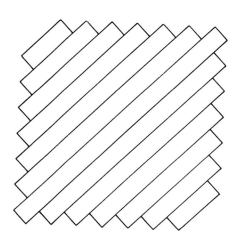

Lone Star Quilt

Quilt Size – 68" x 68"
Template – Small
Diamonds per row – 8
Strip Width – 2¼"

Reverse-Repeat Design Cutting Instructions

Fabric	Amount	Template Methods		Strip Method	
		Rows to Cut	Diamonds in Each	Strips to Cut	Size 2¼" x
1	¼ yard	16	1	16	6½"
2	⅜	16	2	16	10"
3	½	16	3	16	13"
4	½	16	4	16	16"
5	⅝	16	5	16	19"
6	¾	16	6	16	22½"
7	⅞	16	7	16	25½"
8	1	8	8	8	28½"

Repeat Design Cutting Instructions

Fabric	Amount	Template Methods Cut 8 rows of 8 diamonds from each fabric	Strip Method Cut 8 pieces in each size 2¼" x
		Separate into smaller rows of diamonds (Diamonds in each)	
1	1 yard	1 / 7	6½" / 25½"
2	of	2 / 6	9½" / 22½"
3	each	3 / 5	13" / 19"
4		4 / 4	16" / 16"
5		5 / 3	19" / 13"
6		6 / 2	22½" / 9½"
7		7 / 1	25½" / 6½"
8		8	28½"

Radiating Design Cutting Instructions

Fabric	Amount	Template Methods Cut 8 rows from each fabric (Diamonds in each)	Strip Method Cut 8 strips from each fabric 2¼″ x
1 & 15	¼ yard	1	6½″
2 & 14	⅜	2	10″
3 & 13	½	3	13″
4 & 12	½	4	16″
5 & 11	⅝	5	19″
6 & 10	¾	6	22½″
7 & 9	⅞	7	25½″
8	1	8	28½″

Sewing Layouts

Background – 2 yards
Borders – 1½ yards
Backing – 9 yards
Binding – 1½ yards

Template Methods

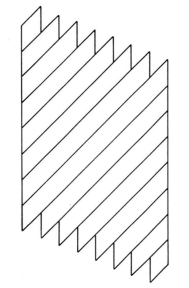

Strip Method

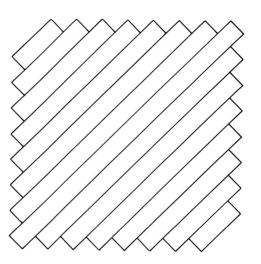

Lone Star Quilt

Quilt Size – 65″ x 65″
Template – Tiny
Diamonds per row – 9
Strip Width – 2″

Reverse-Repeat Design Cutting Instructions

Fabric	Amount	Template Methods		Strip Method	
		Rows to Cut	Diamonds in Each	Strips to Cut	Size 2″ x
1	¼ yard	16	1	16	6″
2	¼	16	2	16	9″
3	⅜	16	3	16	11½″
4	½	16	4	16	14½″
5	⅝	16	5	16	17½″
6	⅝	16	6	16	20″
7	¾	16	7	16	23″
8	⅞	16	8	16	26″
9	1	8	9	8	29″

Repeat Design Cutting Instructions

Fabric	Amount	Template Methods Cut 8 rows of 9 diamonds from each fabric — Separate into smaller rows of diamonds (Diamonds in each)	Strip Method Cut 8 pieces in each size 2″ x
1	1 yard	1 / 8	6″ / 26″
2	of	2 / 7	9″ / 23″
3	each	3 / 6	11½″ / 20″
4		4 / 5	14½″ / 17½″
5		5 / 4	17½″ / 14½″
6		6 / 3	20″ / 11½″
7		7 / 2	23″ / 9″
8		8 / 1	25½″ / 6″
9		9	29″

Radiating Design Cutting Instructions

Fabric	Amount	Template Methods Cut 8 rows from each fabric (Diamonds in each)	Strip Method Cut 8 strips from each fabric 2″ x
1 & 17	¼ yard	1	6″
2 & 16	¼	2	9″
3 & 15	⅜	3	11½″
4 & 14	½	4	14½″
5 & 13	⅝	5	17½″
6 & 12	⅝	6	20″
7 & 11	¾	7	23″
8 & 10	⅞	8	26″
9	1	9	29″

Sewing Layouts

Background–2 yards
Borders–1¼ yards
Backing–5 yards
Binding–1¼ yards

Template Methods

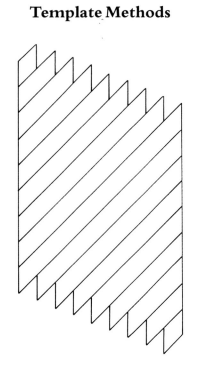

Strip Method

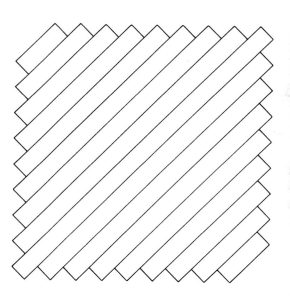

Broken Star Wall/Baby Quilt

Quilt Size – 44" x 44"
Template – Tiny
Diamonds per row – 3
Strip Width – 2"

Reverse-Repeat Design Cutting Instructions

Fabric	Amount	Template Methods		Strip Method	
		Rows to Cut	Diamonds in Each	Strips to Cut	Size 2" x
1	½ yard	64	1	64	6"
2	¾	64	2	64	9"
3	½	32	3	32	11½"

Repeat Design Cutting Instructions

Fabric	Amount	Template Methods	Strip Method
		Cut 32 rows of 3 diamonds from each fabric	Cut 32 pieces in each size
		Separate into smaller rows of diamonds (Diamonds in each)	2" x
1	½ yard	1 / 2	6" / 9"
2	of	2 / 1	9" / 6"
3	each	3	11½"

Radiating Design Cutting Instructions

Fabric	Amount	Template Methods	Strip Method
		Cut 32 rows from each fabric	Cut 32 strips from each fabric
		(Diamonds in each)	2" wide x
1 & 5	½ yard	1	6"
2 & 4	¾	2	9"
3	½	3	11½"

Sewing Layouts

	Template Methods	Strip Method

Background – 1¼ yards
Borders – 1½ yards
Backing – 3 yards
Binding – 1 yard

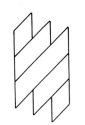

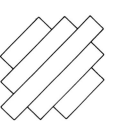

Broken Star Quilt

Quilt Size – 72″ x 72″
Template – Tiny
Diamonds per row – 5
Strip Width – 2″

Reverse-Repeat Design Cutting Instructions

Fabric	Amount	Template Methods		Strip Method	
		Rows to Cut	Diamonds in Each	Strips to Cut	Size 2″ x
1	½ yard	64	1	64	6″
2	¾	64	2	64	9″
3	1	64	3	64	11½″
4	1⅜	64	4	64	14½″
5	1	32	5	32	17½″

Repeat Design Cutting Instructions

Fabric	Amount	Template Methods — Cut 32 rows of 3 diamonds from each fabric. Separate into smaller rows of diamonds (Diamonds in each)	Strip Method — Cut 32 pieces in each size 2″ x
1	1 yard	1 / 4	6″ / 14½″
2	of	2 / 3	9″ / 11½″
3	each	3 / 2	11½″ / 9″
4		4 / 1	14½″ / 6″
5		5	17½″

Radiating Design Cutting Instructions

Fabric	Amount	Template Methods — Cut 32 rows from each fabric (Diamonds in each)	Strip Method — Cut 32 strips from each fabric 2″ wide x
1 & 5	½ yard	1	6″
2 & 4	¾	2	9″
3	½	3	11½″

Sewing Layouts   **Template Methods**   **Strip Method**

Background–2¾ yards
Borders–1½ yards
Backing–9 yards
Binding–1½ yards

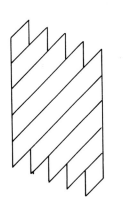
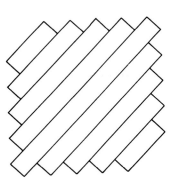

Assembling the Star

Assemble the star, adding eight square background pieces. All stitching should start and end on the sewing line, not the raw edge of the points. Sew the remaining points into groups of three. Sew these to the star, then sew the seams between the groups. Add two triangles to each side. The corners are formed by three squares. They can also be formed with a solid piece or by two pieces with a diagonal seam. Use the measurement of the square to make pattern pieces for these alternatives.

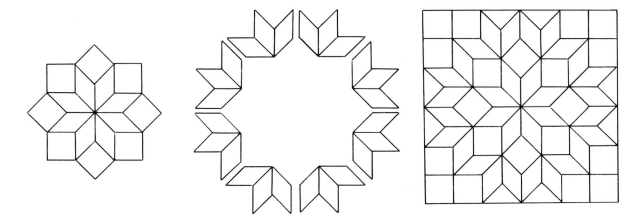

Christmas Wreath

Fabric	Amount	Cutting Instructions
Background	¾ yard	Cut 8 single diamonds
		Cut 8 rows of 2 diamonds
		Cut 8 rows of 5 diamonds
		Cut 8 rows of 6 diamonds
Wreath	½ yard	Cut 8 rows of 3 diamonds
		Cut 8 rows of 4 diamonds

Sewing Layouts   Template Methods

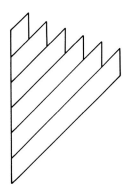

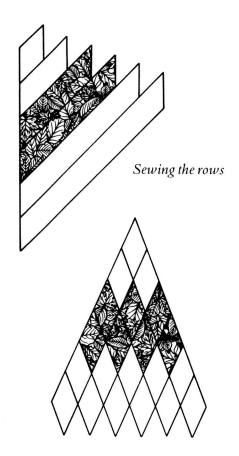

Sewing the rows

Sewing

This festive wreath can be framed in an 18 inch hoop or made into a pillow for the holidays. The background can be solid or a small print. Use a green for the wreath and two shades of red will give the bow dimension. Use the small template, following the Template Method of construction.

Sew into the sewing layout. Cut apart then turn the rows of diamonds over, keeping them in order. Sew into wedge shaped sections. Join the eight sections.

Cut the pieces for the bow from two shades of red. Add a scant ¼ inch seam allowance to all the pieces and hand applique in place.

✳ About the Authors _____

Blanche Young is the innovator of the special cutting and sewing techniques that have changed the way thousands of quilters now make their quilts. Having worked extensively sewing and teaching sewing, she developed steamlined methods which she then applied to patchwork. The publication of the original *Lone Star Quilt Handbook* in 1979 was the culmination of a decade of teaching and researching her methods.

A popular teacher and speaker at quilt conferences across the country, Blanche continues to produce outstanding quilts combining her flair for fabrics and her eye for color. She lives in Westminster, California.

Helen Young Frost became involved with quiltmaking in 1972, and began teaching two years later. She worked with her mother, Blanche Young, developing and refining their methods. She does the writing and illustrations for all their books, and sometimes manages to do some quilts for them too.

Helen is the current (1988-89) president of the American/International Quilt Association. She collects antique quilts and brand-new fabrics. She lives in Tucson, Arizona with her husband, Tom, and children, Sarah, Rebecca and Paul.